At Least 42 Lines

Tania Guruwatte

BookLeaf
Publishing

India | USA | UK

Presentation by *BookLeaf Publishing*

Web: www.bookleafpub.com

E-mail: info@bookleafpub.com

ISBN: 978-93-5744-830-7

First edition 2022

DEDICATION

To Mom and Dad, who are most patiently awaiting the onset of my fame, fortune, and success.

Keep being patient. I love you.

And to Nathan, who was way more stressed out about the deadline than I was.

ACKNOWLEDGEMENT

I acknowledge that I am a writer. This is what I do, and it is what I will continue to do for years to come.

I also acknowledge that this is not the most organized or polished body of work. I digress.

Thanks to everyone who takes the time to read this—or better yet, to find something that they like about it.

PREFACE

These poems were desperately gathered before the deadline from my iPhone notes and poems that I've published as Instagram captions. Oh, and there's a Yelp review in here, too.

Enjoy. Or don't!

The heart is

The heart is a machine—
a pump—
a magnet.
It is a compass,
navigating through stormy seas
and sunny treetops.
The heart is a red bird,
Two superposed subatomic particles,
And an eggshell
floating on one of Saturn's rings.
And at least in one of your lifetimes,
The heart is a cheap motel
with a funny smell
and a bag of chicken wings.

It's day nineteen

It's day nineteen of twenty-one.
Can you say pro-cras-ti-na-tion?

Ceylon tea

Ceylon tea with milk and honey
sipped on a terracotta terrace
with sun-glazed bronze in all its glory:
Shades of me that tell a story.
My eyes are known as Luck and Envy,
reflections of the rolling hills—
effervescent emerald flecks
that do not match the architects'.
My genesis is in the Kumbura,
Goyam Kavi! The crop is golden
like the temple at Dambulla,
like the color of my skin.

Make it

I can't make you go,
and I can't make you stay.
I can't make you show me
the right or wrong way.
I can't make you wish,
and I can't make you pray.
But if I've made you happy,
I've made my whole day.

That time I wrote a Yelp review

My hungry, well-hung, and reasonably hungover partner and I visited the Nashville Jam Café this morning after a night out. We had reached the level of hunger that necessitates a badass breakfast—but not the level of hungover that makes excuses for a bad assbreakfast—so we had respectably mild expectations. Boasting a 4.5 star rating and claiming a menu "sure to please", we figured that by opting for Nashville Jam Café we'd be risking very little for some biscuits.

We walk in and sit down in a sunny corner, a quaint little window seat. Off to a great start. Then, our waitress brings us water in red plastic Solo cups—big frat party energy. Stoked. I order a coffee. Notes of styrofoam and scorn. I get it, you'd have to wash a mug if you served my coffee in one. Must be conserving water. Slowly, we realize that all dining-ware is made of styrofoam and plastic. So they're going for a picnic-y aesthetic. (Side note: If you've never been invited to the cook out for reasons no one will explain to you, this place is for you.) Plus, they can just destroy the evidence— I mean throw our plates and cups and forks and knives away when we're done eating—so no need to hire a dishwasher. Frugal business model that underscores the restaurant's southern appeal. We totally get the theme.

Until we notice two cans of some sort of energy drink placed intentionally on the windowsill. But then again, I sort of get it. Kind of complements the Solo cups. We enjoy questioning the ambiance and peruse the menu, which looks promising. I decide not to order breakfast tacos because we are at a frat party and that would be weird. Nashville hot chicken biscuit it is. He gets the two egg breakfast with a side of sausage gravy for his biscuits. I would typically advise one not to order gravy at a frat party either, but since we are in an establishment that "specializes in New Southern food", maybe it's ok to try new southern things. The waitress asks if we would like jam with our biscuits, and I quickly reply, "sure!" even though I know I probably won't have anything to put the jam on, but for name's sake, you know. This is Nashville's Jam Café.

She doesn't bring any jam. Maybe they ran out
of plastic ramekins to serve it in?

Eggs, grits, bacon looked good upon first
impression. Didn't look like anybody's auntie
made them, but they were clearly going for
picnic here, not cook out. Chicken biscuit didn't
look like the best decision I'd ever made, but I
was optimistic on account of the fact that I had
now reached hunger level: Assbreakfast.

My optimism faded as I partially sunk my teeth
into the chicken breast—it's toughness wouldn't
allow for full tooth sinkage. But who needs
optimism when closure is just a chipped tooth
away? Now I know to ask for tacos at my next
frat party. Hold the gravy. If you take anything at
all from this review, please…let that be it.

The grits were definitely the worst I've ever had,
but my optimism returned as I realized that they
were also definitely the best item on the table. I
took two bites and one more sip of scornful
styrofoam before our waitress returned to ask,
"How was everything?", to which I casually
replied, "It wasn't good", but she probably
already knew that. She didn't say anything
back— not even "I know"—and offered us our

check. She seemed to be well-versed in "new
southern" hospitality.

I would give this restaurant a 5-star rating
because
1. It seems like that's what everyone else is
doing and
2. The experience led us immediately to Waffle
House afterwards and
3. Primed us for the most grateful small diner
moment of our lives.

If you've never been to Waffle House, you
should go!

Distant

This morning I pined
for sunlight cascading gently between the blinds
to kiss your face
before I reached you with
my own lips—
my own beam.
This morning I find
a silent recollection
of my own dream—
a still, somnolent hum
that quietly yearns
for your rhythm.

Half the brain

If I had half the brain today
That I had yesterday,
Well, then I'd say
I'm moving in the wrong direction.
Wait!
Going the wrong way.

Dusty boxes

Fear and uncertainty
are natural deviations
coexisting with
optimism and patience.
I am not, by nature,
perfectly self-assured.
As I grow into myself,
I notice things—
the things I have in common with
the woman who
turns her attention dismissively
from the male gaze,
With the man who
fills voids of an unforgiving lifetime
with dusty boxes stacked
with odd means to an end,
With the widow who
drinks tea religiously by the window
as she is stalked by memories looming outside.

For Medgar

I've arrived
late for the party,
skin frost-bitten with evocation,
ears attuned to chilling echos
in the wind.
None of this looks like you:
Barren, white
None of it feels like you:
Frosty, frigid
None of this is you, my friend,
but the souvenirs of your laughter,
your kindness and hospitality
remind me of where I am—
remind me of where I've always been.

So do I

You deserve to be loved
by someone like me.
But so do I,
in that capacity.

Inhibition

Standing nude
in a dollhouse window,
I wondered how I must appear.
I stepped outside to see myself,
and yes, the curtains—
they are sheer—
Perhaps that isn't what I fear.

Elberta girl

An act of violence
Begets
Vehement regret
And posthumous pain,
Fear, disdain
A shadow that bleeds, leaks
As you tiptoe and laugh
And dance in the street,
Carnation skirt cascading in
Circles of a buoyant spin—
360 degrees of unencumbered bliss.
You are the reason the world
Keeps turning.
You are the Axis.
So may I ask this?
How may I translate your twirls
In a way that reaches
The outermost stars and planets?
I, like you
Wish to
Pirouette and glide
And guide the praxis.

Invitation

She invited me this morning
to come in from the cold
and marvel at her winter wardrobe
In all its periwinkle splendor.
She played me a song on
her technicolor xylophone,
and the notes tickled my ears like sea spray,
unequivocally condemning crushed and bitter,
Fortifying me
in a thick, marshmallow whisper:
Watch all, See all.
Love all, Be all.

To my parents on Valentine's Day

Anyone who I've ever loved
Owes gratitude to you
For kneading with liberal tenderness
And into me the ways of affection,
Of compassion,
Of forgiveness,
For stretching the gum of my gumption
Just ever so much
With caution lest you redesign my composition,
For providing a mirror of warm memories to
bask in,
For if not knowing, then asking,
For giving me a tongue that speaks when it
suffers
And eyes that seek to find others,
For being the boat,
Moved by the force of all I am becoming,
For demonstrating that life goes on,
For life goes on
For loving.

Waking up next to you

Waking up next to you is like molasses—
Warm, sweet, and leisurely,
Dripping in sensual amber tones,
Supple skin and solid bones,
Alone.
Greeting the day from my humble home,
My temple.

Colorblind

I thought I could color your world
With the sherbet hues of the sunrise,
The lavenders and blues of the morning dew,
The pale yellow kiss of the moonlight.
I thought that my voice was enough,
'Cause it's made of that indigo stuff
With ribbons of rouge to offset the cool
Tones dissolving like vinegared rust.
My slate-jade eyes couldn't find you,
Because you swallowed their gaze in small sips.
My cinnamon skin couldn't bind you,
Nor could my rose petal lips.
In leaving the color behind you,
Absence is the pigment you choose.
If only I could remind you
Of the once-lovely palette you used...

A letter to my dear Atlantic

Don't be fretful.
Do not panic!
Don't be bitter, salty sea,
For soon, I shall return to thee.
I've met another, to be specific.
If I recall, his name's Pacific.
I'm captivated currently—
But still, I will return to thee.
Our bond is tried, true, and organic...
So do not panic!

Dandelion

Modest buds of golden hue
Call to Nature's fertile lips
To sip the sun and morning dew
'Til gentle wind tenders her kiss.

Loss is

Loss is loss
As ashes are dust
And the ocean is the sea.
It isn't yours,
As I've been sold,
But it does not belong to me.
Loss is loss,
As ice is frost,
And as happiness is glee.
It's no coin-toss,
No tournament,
No cutthroat rivalry.
So keep in mind,
As darkness blinds
And light will help you see,
Loss will do as loss does.
Loss will simply be.

Roach fantasy (inspired by D.C. Young Fly)

Once I was chillin', I saw a roach.
I said,
"STOP right there, do not approach.
Please don't come close,
'cause I will deliver!!!
You 'bout to get split by my size 8 slipper!!"
I took off my shoe and went in for the attack, but
the roach came through with a clap back, tried to
react fast—
But the b**** grew wings, flew down to the
floor, ran out the door—
Before I could pursue him, he came back with
more!
A whole roach party!
Nah, a roach army.
That's when I realized there was no hope for me,
So I said,
"Y'all roaches make yourselves at home.
Just save me the crumbs from your
Honeycombs."

A quatrain I wrote when I was 9 that still lives in my head rent free

We were both fighting
Over a blanket.
She pulled, I kicked.
She tugged, I yanked it.

9 789357 448307